Better than Credit Repair

Third edition copyright © 2008, 2012, 2015 Tamara Rasheed

ISBN 10: 1505842824

ISBN 13: 978-1-5058-4282-1

Published by Tamara Rasheed, Michigan

Design and layout by Tamara Rasheed

Printed in the United States of America

Table of Contents

Acknowledgments

Like most books, this one is certainly a labor of love. The writing of this book came at a time in my life when I thought I was most beaten, most fractured, and with the largest amount of struggles. I was on my way out of an abusive marriage with 3 children and nowhere to go, no income, and what I thought was bad credit. Fortunately, I was able to turn my skills as a credit specialist into a gateway to new hope. I rose as my credit skills rose in life and I was truly able to see what people needed - someone who cared, someone who was knowledgeable, and someone who was willing to share what they knew.

My desire to persevere has been given to me – along with many other amazing blessings – by God. I owe my thanks to Him first and foremost for giving me patience, letting me cry and keep going, and giving me the information I needed to make a life for my children.

Secondly, I want to thank everyone who believed in me, cheered me on, gave me hugs and wiped my tears. There are people you meet along the journey of life who remind you of where you've been, where you are and where you can go. I've been blessed with many people like these – some temporary and some lasting.

Thank you for all of your support - you know who you are.

This book is dedicated
to all of you who have lived the most difficult
lives all because you weren't provided the knowledge
you needed to overcome common difficulties
with your finances:

Becoming comfortable and surviving is just a start.
It's knowing that you have greater goals than survival
that makes it possible to begin living the life of your dreams.

A goal is a dream with ACTION behind it!

Preface

As I work with clients from across the United States, I see the same worries, the same struggles and the same fears. As adults we need a certain amount of nurturing too. We need validation. We need to know that we can do better than what we have done and progress further than where we have come. Some of the individuals I work with are familiar with reading their personal credit reports and working with companies that send out dispute letters on their behalf. They know all about making payment arrangements and settlements and addressing mistakes they've made with their finances, but what comes next? What are the steps that prevent mistakes in the future and what are the little known secrets that prevent you from losing your peace of mind when it comes to your credit? We realize the power of credit after mistakes have already been made. We didn't go to school to learn about credit. There was no home study course or any way to find out what you're getting into outside of your own failures. Using your credit never seems to lead to the relief that you're building a lifestyle. Instead, it's one more thing that takes money out of your pocket. This creates a serious disability because it is difficult to be a part of a functioning society without good credit.

As we grow and become independent, we begin living life

the best way we know how. Wisdom tells us to learn from the mistakes of others, but we typically tell ourselves that experiencing our own mistakes is the best way to go. I don't know about you, *but if I had a resource of other people's mistakes that was candidly laid out for me*, I would have been far more likely to study them before trying to go it alone and less likely to make some of the costly mistakes I had to face in my young adulthood. Unfortunately, the rest of our lives are spent trying to recover from the mistakes we've made, as we are unable to live the quality of life that we imagined living.

Choosing to experience a bad decision in order to experience a mistake, *when there are already examples of that bad decision all around you*, is insane. It isn't smart, or wise, or necessary. Expecting to find a different result when YOU experience that mistake, as if no one else grew up and learned how to take care of themselves but you, is the same as doing the same things expecting a different result. This is the definition of insanity!

When you look at other credit books, you can find all of the advice you would ever want to follow, but they are missing one thing – the acknowledgment of your mistakes so that you don't make them again. I am a human being like anyone else. I made my mistakes so that you don't have to. But I also broke the cycle of making those mistakes so that I could live a better life and show others how to do it also.

I call this book The Handbook of Credit Mastery because no matter where you are in your credit journey, it meets you in that place and helps you to overcome the obstacles to become successful. You can master your OWN personal credit for what YOU want it to create for you. I candidly share my story in this book so that you know I have made mistakes *and have overcome them.* I provide you all of the tools that I've used over the years that have brought me success – including tools that created multiple streams of income for me to offset the fact that my job didn't always provide what I needed alone.

This book is about progressing beyond where you are and stopping a pattern in it's tracks. Whether you're recovering your credit from misuse or misfortune, learning how to build your credit for the first time, or upgrading your credit to purchase assets, you will find what you are looking for here. In this book you will discover that even if you haven't had problems with your credit in the past, there is still *one vital thing* missing from your approach to credit that will always keep you *just over broke.* This *one thing* is what makes this process – the development of your personal credit – *Better Than Credit Repair.*

This book has been created to empower you. You will find tools, worksheets, examples and a clear path to follow toward your goals that you can accomplish on your own.

This handbook will cover in great detail how one of the fundamental principles of the development of credit is proper credit card use. While many of us have become afraid to use credit cards because of impending debt, the debt is not what causes issues. Your lack of a basic credit knowledge base to teach you how to use credit cards properly before you get one has set you up for failure. The credit card itself is not at fault.

Credit card use is the easiest way to raise your credit scores dramatically if you use them the right way. Since this book is dedicated to using personal credit as a valuable resource, learning how to use credit cards the right way, as well as separating the terms "credit cards" from "credit" as a whole is just a natural part of this system. This is only one of the valuable principles that you will learn as you progress through this book.

What are we supposed to be using credit for? Why is credit so important? How do I properly care for my credit? These questions create the backdrop and motivation for an excellent credit lifestyle. When you understand why credit exists and how it affects you on a personal level, then you will better understand how to care for it and maintain it properly.

The hardest people to care for are your loved ones because they do not always respect your opinion, and they do not always take heed to your advice. If Better Than Credit Repair: The Handbook of Credit Mastery can have a nationwide effect on the way credit is understood and used, then you will not need to convince them. The current state of our credit economy, and the fact that they learned about their credit from mistakes, or the fact that they haven't learned how to use credit from any credible or qualified source that can guarantee excellence, should be proof enough.

Read this book and become comfortable in the fact that mistakes have already been made. You are now becoming wise for seeing those mistakes elsewhere and learning a qualified method of success for your credit wellbeing from this point forward.

Author

Introduction

My first credit card came in an unmarked envelope. I was 17 years old at the time and as I marveled at the beauty of the little plastic card with my name on it, it dawned on me that it might have a potential greater than I realized. I asked my mother what I should do to take care of it, and she responded, "Pay your bills on time." And shortly after, I ran away from home.

My teenage years were troubled, riddled with self doubt, low self esteem, unanswered questions and being unsure about my place in the world. It didn't take much to become one of 1.6 – 2.8 million youth who run away from home each year. I was the textbook case of teenage depression, but I wasn't the textbook teenager. I had been a college student since the age of 13, called the "Doogie Houser" of education because I walked around with a brief case and was mistaken as someone's child in every class. I had a difficult time connecting with others and fitting in and I needed guidance. My parents did the best they could for me, but our communication needed a lot of work. I connected with an older man on the internet – a parent's worst nightmare – and one day, I disappeared.

While I won't disclose everything I went through, abruptly leaving home with my family desperately looking for me, identity theft was one of the traumatic events that stuck with me far after I came home.

Before I was able to create the opportunity to make plans for my credit, someone else made plans, making my credit unusable and leaving me with debt that didn't belong to me. I fell victim to an internet predator who was looking for a naïve, heartbroken young girl to take advantage of. He stole checks from my check book, created a fake driver's license, opened accounts at department stores, financed appliances, furniture and electronics all in my name. Although I was eventually found and was able to come back home, the humiliation of leaving home and being taken advantage of continued to plague me. I became withdrawn, and continued problems pushed me out of the nest early. Before I knew it, I was married at the age of 18 to a 19 year old husband.

My husband and I were young. Pressure from my parents to get married created later resentment. We were not equipped with the tools we needed to get to know one another and sustain our lives together, let alone nurture a new, young marriage. We already felt like we were taking on the world's problems without a clue. The pressure of our finances and soon, a baby, created the fuel our marriage needed to crash and burn. After only 14 months, I was a single parent and a divorcee at the age of 20. As I wondered if things could get any worse, sitting at a red light on a Sunday morning before I turned 21, wondering where I wanted my life to go and feeling hopeless, I was hit head on by a speeding driver. I had internal injuries, a broken nose, my pelvic bone was broken in two, and my face was so swollen my little boy didn't recognize me and cried when he was left alone with me. The medical bills that I incurred only added to my devastated credit and fractured self esteem.

I am sharing my story with you as a gateway into how unpredictable life can be. Trauma of all kinds causes scars and it doesn't discriminate based on age. Every mistake we make creates a scar in our lives. These scars are reminders that mistakes hurt and that we were not as prepared or as responsible as we wanted to be. At the same time, those mistakes and scars make us who we are. I can look back on where I have been and be grateful for those experiences because they created the foundation for being able to protect myself and my children against the same types of mistakes in the future.

Identity theft was my gateway into learning more about my credit. Even though you have suffered misfortunes in life and made mistakes, they happened so that you can learn from them in order to avoid those same mistakes in the future. I know now to protect my credit and my finances, not to trust people I don't know with my personal information or my person, and to monitor what my credit is doing. I learned that credit repair means that once you've broken your credit, you can find a fix for it. My credit wasn't broken or unusable, but my knowledge about credit led me to believe that it was. Admittedly, I really didn't know anything about credit at all, but I did know that when I filled out an application for a credit card or a car or anything else that I wanted, I was denied. That was pretty broken to me. There are several problems with this mindset. The first problem is that "breaking" your credit is inevitable. The proverbial "they" are sure that your credit will become broken. The second problem is that this thing, your credit, that you have have your entire life, has no way to protect itself from becoming broken and you will have to seek out a repair service eventually. Like a computer with no virus software, waiting for a problem to strike. There is an entire business built around knowing your credit is going to "break". Third, if you can fix it, that means eventually it can become irreparable. That there will come a point where you will never be able to use your credit again because you just can't fix that big mistake.

Most of us suffer from traumatic events where we have to make difficult financial decisions. Our parents become elderly and we have to use our income to offset theirs. Suddenly bills begin to go to collections and we have to ignore the bills that aren't as important. Natural disasters, job loss, medical emergencies, divorce, identity theft and countless other circumstances put our finances in jeopardy all the time, and put our basic needs in danger.

There is an age old saying that goes, "A fool learns from his mistakes, and the wise man learns from the mistakes of others." I am handing you all of my mistakes for you to study. My mistakes allowed me to look for a way out and provide purpose to my life. Because I was able to do that for myself, I can help you to do the same thing. I will help you overcome your past mistakes, create a plan for what you want to build in your life, and allow you to get the things you want by mastering the purpose of your own personal credit through this book. You now have the opportunity to give your credit life.

Instead of looking at my credit as this fractured, helpless thing in need of repair, I choose to look at it the way I look at my health. I may be unhappy with my health today, but I know that I can make a plan that will make it better in the coming weeks. Eating right, exercising, taking the stairs instead of the elevator are all little things I can do to make a big difference in my health today. Credit isn't any different. There are techniques you can use daily, weekly and monthly to make sure that you can make a difference in your credit standing, no matter how bad you feel it is today.

Credit quick fixes and incomplete advice can only take you so far. "Pay your bills on time" didn't prepare me for the worst. It also couldn't describe the potential my credit could allow me to achieve either. If I spent the same amount of time learning how to build an income with GOOD debt that I spent on making mistakes, I could have received an income each month from money working for me – a permanent protection for everything I was working hard for. But it wasn't too late for me. And it isn't too late for you.

When it comes to credit, the major focus has always been

on failure!

There is an endless sea of "credit repair" and "credit improvement" companies out there, and the purpose of this action based guide is to not only cut through the sea of bad advice and what doesn't work but to provide you with the guidance that you need as a one-on-one consultant on the development of your personal credit toward your goals.

Look at what happens when you search for "credit repair" online:

Results 1 - 10 of about 31,600,000 for credit repair. (0.21 seconds)

How are you supposed to accurately choose from over *31 million* results for the best way to manage your credit?

The amount of credit repair companies only stands to become larger as the credit economy worsens and more and more people emerge without any kind of credit knowledge base at all.

One of the first things we need to change in our credit vocabulary is the association of credit with "repair."

The nature of credit is not of something that breaks and needs to be fixed. You have your credit for your entire life. It is something that is flexible and is always with you – just like your health. Credit always has the potential to be excellent, no matter where it is currently. Just like your health, if you don't care for it properly, it becomes ill, and remedies are necessary to get it back to where it should be.

Credit always fluctuates. It goes up and down – *if* you don't know how to control it. Positive and negative accounts are added to your credit and taken away all the time, and the key is to understand how credit works so that we can control what our credit is doing at all times.

The standard market price for "credit repair" services is $500. Any company or individual with any kind of credit knowledge will tell you to make deletions, dispute inaccuracies, and update your personal information. $500 is a lot of money to dish out for a basic and temporary "fix" for your credit woes!

The focus of credit repair businesses, and the mainstream credit economy for the lower middle class and middle class, is to only pay attention to things when they fail, and that is *wrong*.

Another serious problem is that the major goal of most people is to become "just a little less high risk" in their credit approvability.

We no longer live in a society where approval is difficult to get. Funders, lenders and creditors approve most people across the board, because preying on individuals who have low credit scores is more lucrative. Sufferers of bad and uncertain credit spend thousands and thousands of dollars over what they are supposed to be spending just for the sake of wanting to be approved.

Fair, Isaac Corporation (FICO) is a third party company, outside of the three major credit bureaus, located in California. They specialize in weighing different factors about your credit behavior to create a scoring model that is widely used between most funders, lenders and other institutions. These are your FICO scores and they are tabulated according to the largest three credit bureaus. There are thousands of credit bureaus that tabulate different factors about your credit and who have their own credit scoring systems. This is why you should not look for or rely on a "credit score."

Credit scores are offered on a 300 – 950 scale and are created by the credit bureaus themselves and not an independent company like FICO. This credit score was created to rival the FICO score that is more widely used. Credit scores give individuals a false idea of what their credit is doing. How? By tabulating different factors than the factors necessary for having prime credit across the board according to FICO. Why? Because consumers with excellent credit have lower interest rates, save thousands of dollars per year with less fees and charges, and the credit bureaus don't make as much money when you make good decisions.

It is merely the credit bureau's way of detouring you from improving your FICO scores and lowering your interest rates so that they can protect the profit they are making on your bad credit behaviors.

FICO rates your credit score on a scale from 400 – 850, 400 being the worst and 850 being excellent.

High Risk 619

Uncertain 620 to 660

Acceptable (average) 661 to 720

Very good 721 or higher

Excellent over 750

The real problem isn't our approvability; the problem is our ability to develop our credit to average, good and excellent so that our interest rates either start out low, or eventually become low.

The ability to develop prime credit is the difference between a car note of $199 per month, and a car note of $700 per month for the same year, make and model of car. It is the difference between an interest rate of 6% or 11% on our mortgage payments. It is the difference between a 9.9% interest rate for the life of a credit card, and an interest rate of 25 – 35% on the life of a credit card. People who do not have the income to afford this loss give literally THOUSANDS of dollars away each year. These people lack a dependable way to manage their credit and pay their bills to their ultimate benefit as an ideal borrower instead of to their immediate gratification – just to keep your lights on and your car in your driveway. That is what protection is for!

Beyond approvability, we need to create ways to build credit resources so that we can purchase assets to protect our basic needs.

I have a friend, who I will keep going back to as an example, who is very close to me and works 80+ hours per week. He has a young son and is constantly going through marital problems.

He and his wife care for their basic needs between both of their incomes. He has an industrial job that wears heavily on him, their credit is in the 700s, they are debt free, but have no current credit debts on file – they basically have unestablished credit with a 700 score because they have no current credit history. They also have no credit resources or assets.

My friend, unfortunately, is the perfect client for a predator who wants to approve him for the highest interest rate possible with expensive payments that can ruin his credit standing altogether.

What would happen if my friend got hurt on his job and couldn't work, or if he and his wife actually got a divorce and suddenly incurred debt?

This is what living on the brink of disaster is like.

Most of us live on the brink of disaster *just like he does.* We work, but have no credit history, no assets to back up our income and no recourse when things go wrong.

The credit economy we live in is geared toward approving as many people as possible, because the worse off your credit is, the higher interest rates you will be charged, not to mention the hidden fees and other charges that apply. **This is how the credit industry makes their money!**

Don't get me wrong, paying interest on money you borrow through credit is absolutely fair. You are asking someone to loan you money, *but* you should be equipped with the skills necessary to upgrade your credit to the optimum level – 750 to

850 – so that you can reduce the amount of interest you pay.

Without a proper credit knowledge base, we follow the rules that the credit industry lays out for us without question.

For example, we are told to make our payments on time although by doing that, we make payments on the brink of disaster.

No one asks the question "If I make my payments on time and something happens, doesn't that make my payments automatically late? Doesn't that put me in danger of losing what I have?"

If we suffer an unforeseen situation – lose a job, divorce a spouse, or suffer suddenly from a serious medical illness – we become unable to sustain our basic needs, and the lack of protection and security puts us into bad credit debt!

But are those situations really unseen? We look around us and those same situations are the stories of the people we love, the people we work with and the people who live nearby us. Wouldn't it make more sense to have a plan in place incase anything like that were to happen to us?

As another example, Experian was able to take away public access of their FICO score from every forum available to individuals in the United States in 2014. While they began offering their FICO score again in 2015, they made it clear that individuals are not the customers of the credit bureaus - the lenders are!

A law was also passed that prevents the individual from

receiving their FICO scores at the same time their credit reports are pulled. Tactics like these prevent the likelihood that an individual would not apply for credit because of their credit scores.

This is the very reason why the Fair Credit Reporting Act was instituted - to protect consumers from being victimized by credit companies - but there is no act that provides us with control by allowing us to view our FICO scores before we apply for credit!

Trans Union and Equifax could follow the same route that Experian did, and we wouldn't be able to do anything about it, although we are the most affected by the credit bureau's decisions.

So how do we learn what to do to establish, restore or upgrade our credit to excellent credit, while getting the tools we need to acquire credit resources and credit assets?

This book is an action-based guide developed to answer these questions and more!

Credit Awareness

The best thing you can do for yourself today is to begin learning what the importance of credit truly is. Make a commitment to learn not only its general importance, but the importance you need it to have for your life. We usually know credit from the standpoint of credit scores and reports, credit cards and debt, but do you really know what the importance of credit truly is? Do you know the power of using other people's money? Even if your end goal is not to become wealthy, you can still use credit to create an income for yourself that is independent of what you bring in from your job. Mastering your own personal credit is about becoming aware of the resources that are available to you. What resources will you need to build the vision of your financial future?

Your ability to take care of your basic needs, create a nest egg that can become your retirement, and begin building the lifestyle you want instead of struggling paycheck to paycheck is all at the tip of your fingers with the use of credit. It isn't meant to create more problems and debts for you. What vision do you have for your financial life? Did you know that credit can be the stepping stone you need to get there without having to struggle for years to put money away? Most of your ability to get ahead relies on your money's ability to grow at a speed much faster than working for dollars will allow. Your job is finite and so is your life. There are only so many usable hours that you have in your life. Are you really meant to spend those usable hours trading them for dollars or are you meant to be using dollars to do that work for you? Let's demystify credit by getting a better picture of what it is and how you can use it to work for you.

What is the importance of having credit?

Before we answer this question, we have to focus on what credit really is. Credit, in its most basic sense, is an arrangement that you make that allows you to use money now and pay it back over time.

Credit is important because it creates valuable resources right away that you would not have access to by using your money alone.

Credit is also called "other people's money" because it is something that you borrow or borrow against in order to create additional money that you did not have. Banks lend credit in the form of credit lines.

Without credit, it is very difficult to obtain a higher standard of living, and it is even more difficult to hang onto that higher standard of living once you get it.

What am I trying to prove by having credit anyway?

Credit proves that you have integrity and credibility in your finances. It proves that you can be trusted!

Credit provides a basis of belief for a company or individual seeking to loan you either money or other resources. It tells them that you will be responsible enough to take care of your business relationships.

The rules of building a relationship with a lender or funder are the same in credit as they are in a personal relationship. When you establish credit, it is important for you to build a foundation of financial integrity and credibility, or trust.

This kind of trust allows you to put your money to other uses that actually add to your income, such as in the acquisition of assets or when you save to create collateral. When you create collateral and assets, the use of money to purchase things outright is no longer necessary, and allows you to use a credit for the amount of money you intend to use instead – this means that your money always stays in tact and allows it to grow. This creates the ability to sustain a lifestyle, and secures your basic needs.

Isn't having credit the same as being in debt?

Repayment of any resource that you borrow to use over time is called owing a debt. This is not restricted to credit. If you borrow your friend's lawn mower, you owe him a debt which is payable by giving what you borrowed back, and even returning the favor with loaning him something of yours. When your friend allowed you to borrow his lawnmower, he opened up a channel of trust that created an environment where it is comfortable to lend and borrow between you.

When you owe on a credit debt, It means that you have made a promise to pay back what you are borrowing, which is a responsible thing to do. Plus you promise to pay a profit to whom you are borrowing from for allowing you to borrow that money, which is fair not to expect them to lend you their money for nothing. For example, if you borrow $5,000, and 6% of interest is added to that, you owe a total of $5,300 to the person or entity you borrowed from.

When a person or entity has enough money to lend out for a profit, that person or entity is also called an investor (a person who invests their money into other people. Investors make a profit by charging interest on top of the money they lend.

When a person or entity loans you money, they trust you in your ability to pay them back based in part on your credit profile, and they are taking the risk of not getting back what they loaned to you. Your ability to responsibly care for the business relationship that you built creates credibility and integrity for you.

When a person obtains credit and does not know how to maintain that credit properly, and/or does not have cash enough or cash consistently to maintain that credit, and/or has not built the proper foundation of resources that would allow the maintenance of that credit in the midst of disaster, the foundation of *bad credit debt* has been established.

I highlighted "bad credit debt" and not the words "bad credit." Your credit itself isn't bad, you have just collected bad debts that need to be addressed. And you have established bad habits that may cause future debts to also become bad.

When a person obtains credit with the knowledge necessary for the maintenance of that debt, with cash enough and cash consistently to maintain that credit, and has built the proper foundation of resources that would allow the maintenance of that credit in the midst of disaster, the foundation of *good credit debt* has been established.

The objective here is to establish a foundation of good credit behaviors to create good debt because this foundation will build the necessary resources, collateral and assets that you need for your wellbeing.

So, yes, having credit is having debt – but is it good debt, or bad debt that you are taking on?

At one point, credit was your ability to look a person in the eye, give a person a handshake, write your signature on a contract or IOU or give your word. People no longer have that kind of honor on a mainstream basis, and your credit profile is the best way to determine how you honor your business relationships today. Having bad credit is like someone spreading a rumor about you. It is tarnishing your good name. Bad credit is the tarnishing of your good name in business.

Now that you know what credit is for, its time to focus on any credit illnesses you have so that you can begin work on the building of proper credit resources!

Credit Health

Good credit has to begin outside of your FICO scores in order to affect your FICO scores. I am sure you're not used to hearing that a person with bad credit scores can actually have good credit habits. Sometimes all you need to focus on is not using your credit when you're facing some challenges in your life.

If you seek out other resources when you've hit hard times, then you won't have to worry about fixing your credit after you recover. Sometimes just that realization alone is good credit. Having good credit means that you have the good habits, behaviors and schedules necessary to create a positive impact on your FICO scores. You have to be able to look past your short term situation and consider that you have other needs that will make maintaining credit balances too challenging. If your current bills fall behind, then you should not add credit to this mix. This means that good credit starts long before you see it reflected in your FICO scores. Credit behaviors are an action, and excellent FICO scores are the consequence of that action.

What kinds of behaviors are you showing daily, weekly and monthly that are creating a foundation of bad credit for you? Are you filling out applications for credit cards when the credit cards you currently have are in collections or have high utilizations? Are you looking for the next thing you can finance when your job income is barely enough to meet your everyday needs?

Bad credit, just like good credit, is all about the behaviors that you have committed to. Have you committed to behaviors that will encourage good results or have you unconsciously committed to behaviors that are not serving you? The good news is that you can decide at any time to commit to the right behaviors in order to create the results you're looking for.

Credit Health is the ability to create schedules and habits that encourage the proper maintenance, monitoring and management of your credit profile.

How we pay our bills, buy gas, buy food at a fast food restaurant or pick up necessities for our home provides a greater benefit than what we think it does. If we choose to look at those things as necessary evils, then they will be exactly that – necessary, and evil to our wallet.

Credit Health is about choosing to look at those necessary, consistent purchases as a springboard for your finances to use. Not all of these purchases will be able to fit with your credit profile, but the ones that do will help you to achieve your dreams. Paying for these particular purchases in a particular way, on a particular, easy schedule creates substantial and lightening quick growth for your FICO scores, while creating a picture of positive credit behavior that is current and consistent.

Using the fact that these things have to be paid daily, weekly and monthly on a consistent basis will provide a major benefit for your finances by establishing a reliable payment schedule that will build other resources.

You're probably thinking that there is nothing currently wrong with the way you pay your bills and make these other payments in your life.

You're probably right if your goal is to maintain and survive in your current lifestyle.

Remember, we have been talking about creating a fundamental credit knowledge base for building, developing and upgrading credit. If you're reading this book to find out how to do those things properly, based on the development of credit, then you will need to take my advice. If you're happy with your credit standing and the way your finances currently are working for you, then keep doing what you've been doing! (What are you reading this book for?)

BUT, don't make your payments the same way you've been making them, thinking that it will produce a different or greater result!

Look at your previous five years. Ten years. For as far back as you've been making payments the way you've been making them. What you've already gotten is the most that you're going to continue to get by doing the same thing. (Remember the definition of insanity?)

I wouldn't be talking about bill payments if it wasn't vital, essential, for the growth of your credit.

There is a way to maintain consistency in paying your bills while building an amazing credit resource in the process. In short, do not expect to develop your personal credit and continue to pay your bills in a way that will not produce a greater benefit than you're used to.

When you do not have the proper schedules and habits necessary to encourage excellent credit, it can be called a credit illness! The first thing you need to do is create an organized list of all of the payments that you have to make toward your bills.

Make a copy of the next page to begin tracking your credit payments. Make multiple sheets or use your own bill management software to keep track of your monthly payments. Everything that you pay for monthly should have a category.

Credit Debt Worksheet

Mortgage & Home Equity Credit Line Worksheet*

Lender Name	Loan Amount	Interest & Tax	Principal	Original Due Date	New BTCR Due Date

Total Monthly Payment: $_____
Interest Paid This Month: $_____

Car Loan Worksheet

Lender Name	Loan Amount	Interest Rate (%)	Monthly Payment	Original Due Date	New BTCR Due Date

Total Monthly Payment $_____
Interest Paid This Month: $_____

Credit Card Worksheet

Credit Card Name and Type (MC/Visa)	Credit Limit (Line of Credit)	Credit Balance (25%)	Original Due Date	New BTCR Due Date

Keeping worksheets is important because they will help you to create a clear picture of the amount of money you are paying out every month. As your FICO scores go up and your interest rates come down, you will see dramatic savings in these worksheets.

Begin writing down your purchases at the start of the upcoming week. Write down everything you buy, regardless as to how insignificant it may be, with the price next to it for seven days. The purpose of doing this is to track your spending and to find any unnecessary purchases. You could save yourself tremendous money by having more disciplined spending habits.

Using your credit card to make one small $10 purchase per month and then paying off that balance will drive your utilization down quickly, causing your FICO score to raise dramatically. Using your credit card for purchases that you have the cash on hand to cover and then paying your credit card bill each week or twice each week instead of once per month will show the credit card companies that you do not need to use your credit card as income. This boosts your credit scores tremendously by making regular, frequent payments on your credit cards.

A vital part of the maintenance, management and monitoring of your personal credit is keeping worksheets. You are taking special note of the credit debts you are responsible for and making an effort to give your purchases a deeper focus than you have before. The next step is to build your credibility and integrity with these credit companies.

Six Areas of Special Attention:

These six areas of special attention are the habits and schedules you need to establish with your credit debts in order to improve your FICO scores.

You also want to create new due dates 15 days earlier than your original due dates – Remember, it is important to stay away from the brink of disaster by making early payments and not on-time payments!

1. Keep track of your original due dates – These worksheets will help you do this in an organized way. Although you will be using a due date that is two weeks earlier than your original date, you need to keep your original date in mind because it can be changed without notice. A change in these dates could make your payments late! Call those companies one time every three months to check your due dates.

2. Keep 65% of credit card available balances *untouched* - This means that you never spend all of the money on your credit cards. Every month, you only have 35% of your line of credit that is actually usable as a worst case scenario! Treat that 65% as if it doesn't exist, but work harder to spend less than 10% of your credit card's balance. Credit cards are meant to have large lines of credit to help you

purchase assets. The asset pays off the card because in order to be an asset, it has to pay itself off and pay you also.

3. Do not max out your credit cards – Keeping 65% of your available balance will ensure that you do not max out your credit cards. Credit card companies are looking at your spending habits and valuing how your credit card is being utilized. High utilization makes credit card companies the most money, but takes the most money away from you.

4. Use credit cards for purchases that you currently have the cash on hand to cover. This helps to avoid interest by paying directly on your principal while helping you build your credit card to it's highest potential.

5. Do not pay your credit card bill only one time per month – you are using your credit to pay for what you have cash on hand to cover. Because of this, you can stock pile your money weekly, and pay your credit cards up to 4 times per month. This shows that you don't need to use your credit as income, and that you only use your credit for what you have cash to cover. Credit card companies reward you for this responsible behavior!

6. These steps in Credit Health keep you from paying high interest rates and apply your payments directly to the principle - which regular payments usually avoid. This is the "credit game," and by following these schedules it puts you on the winning team!

Bankruptcy

Bankruptcy is often used as a quick-fix to eliminate debt. Since the 2007 recession, millions of people have filed Chapter 7 or Chapter 13 bankruptcy in an attempt to start over again financially. It has been heavily marketed as a way to help individuals create a clean financial slate and recover from financial challenges that have become too overwhelming to budget for.

Why do individuals choose bankruptcy over debt consolidation? If you had an option to potentially wipe out your debt instead of paying it back, it would be far more tempting to get your debt erased versus creating another bill. Often, the stress of not being able to meet financial obligations, worry and guilt over property being repossessed and even jail time can cause individuals to make decisions they would not have made with better planning.

The problem with quick-fixes is that they are often temporary, they do not cover everything you think they would cover, and they can often cause more problems than they solve. Did you know that most bankruptcy requires a payment plan to be paid on time? If you are already having problems paying your bills on time, this could cause additional worry, especially when your creditors are now protected by a court agreement that says you will pay them on time. Also, did you know that in most cases, your property will be appraised and sold in order to pay off any outstanding debts? If you were not prepared to part with any of your assets, you may be surprised that bankruptcy court is a way to please your creditors and not you.

It is important to talk about bankruptcy because many people look to rebuild credit after they have already filed, or they find that it does not solve all of their problems. For many, bankruptcy creates more financial challenges because it is often much more difficult to get approved with it on your credit file. It ensures that your interest rates stay high, that lenders and funders are a lot more picky about providing you approvals, and that you have even more challenges clearing items off of your credit file during the dispute process because creditors now have court protection.

Before we talk about techniques you can begin applying to recover from bankruptcy, it is important to talk about what it doesn't cover if you are considering filing. Congress has determined that there are 19 categories of debts that are not covered under bankruptcy because they violate public policy.

The following debts are considered the most common types of debts that are not discharged during a Chapter 7 bankruptcy:

Certain types of tax claims

Bankruptcy does not cover certain types of tax claims. If you did not file a tax return, the IRS assess taxes on all unfiled returns and these are ineligible to be discharged by bankruptcy. Most tax debts are not able to be discharged. The IRS has a five rule criteria for discharging tax debts and most people do not qualify based upon these five rules.

1. The tax return was filed at least two years ago.
2. The tax assessment is at least 240 days old.
3. The tax return was not fraudulent.
4. The taxpayer is not guilty of tax evasion.
5. The due date for filing a tax return is at least three years ago.

If you are receiving regular calls from the IRS in an attempt to collect taxes you owe, you may be disappointed that your bankruptcy will not cover your tax liabilities.

Debts you forgot to include in the lists and schedules

If some debts come to your attention that possibly could have been included in your bankruptcy claim prior to submitting your list and schedules, you may find out that they cannot be included in your bankruptcy because they were not identified prior to submitting your paperwork.

Debts for spousal or child support or alimony

If you owe and/or are paying spousal support, child support or alimony, these debts are not eligible to be discharged through bankruptcy. This can be challenging because arrearages can be crippling in many circumstances.

Debts for willful and malicious injuries to person or property

These debts are often called criminal restitution or just restitution and after time is served in prison, restitution may be owed. Contact your attorney or review your judgement to see if you will owe restitution upon release. If these debts are not paid, it can be considered a violation of parole and you can go back to jail. Bankruptcy will not discharge restitution and you will need to make these payments to the court or to the victim or injured party.

Debts to government units for fines and penalties

Debts accrued that are to be paid back to the state government that are usually assessed by a judge may be called Responsibility Fees. These fees can be accrued with misdemeanors and can typically be assessed as a result of a traffic stop that finds drugs, driving while under the influence or no insurance while driving to name a few cases. These debts cannot be included in bankruptcy filings.

Debts for most government funded or guaranteed educational loans or benefit overpayments

Pursuing an education can be expensive. Federal financial aid programs provide access to loans to make payment for tuition possible. These loans do not have the same credit criteria for approval as personal loans, making them much easier to obtain. These loans must be repaid after a student has obtained their degree.

In today's career climate, many people have difficulties finding work in the field of their intended career or may change their minds about entering the industry after school is complete, among many other reasons. In other circumstances jobs just do not pay enough to sustain repayment of the loan and the cost of living, leaving former students with high student loan debt.

These debts are not covered by bankruptcy discharge and former students may be disappointed if they pursued bankruptcy to alleviate those debts.

Debts for personal injury caused by the debtor's operation of a motor vehicle while intoxicated

If the debtor was intoxicated and caused personal injury to a someone who sued and won their claim, the debt incurred can be crippling. If the debtor files for bankruptcy with the hope that the debt will be discharged, they will be disappointed to find that the bankruptcy will not cover these types of debts.

Debts owed to certain tax-advantaged retirement plans

Payments intended to secure your retirement can also create debilitating debts for individuals who are low income or fixed income and cannot sustain larger payments as they progress through life. Debts incurred in certain retirement accounts that have certain types of tax-advantages may not be discharged through bankruptcy.

Debts for certain condominium or cooperative housing fees

Housing debts can amount to 50 – 80% of a person's income and when fees associated with housing become difficult to maintain as a result of job loss, medical emergency or any other brink-of-disaster life challenge, these debts can become debilitating. Individuals seeking bankruptcy can be disappointed to find out that the condominium fees that have become unbearable or coop housing fees that have become overwhelming cannot be discharged.

Debts that are included in a Chapter 13 bankruptcy are often discharged after a payment plan has been met according to terms of the court. Debts that are dischargeable under Chapter 13 that are not dischargeable in a Chapter 7 are:

⌈ Debts for willful and malicious injury to property

⌈ Debts incurred to pay non-dischargeable tax obligations

⌈ Debts arising from property settlements in divorce or separation proceedings.

Before you consider filing bankruptcy

Exhaust all other methods of proper budgeting, increasing your own income, and consult with debt counseling and consolidation services. Before you consider filing for bankruptcy, improve on your foundation of financial education skills and consolidate your debts according to what is easy for your budget.

For most people, their financial education needs to be

improved. Proper budgeting solves most debt problems by increasing income and creating a budget to pay debts on time. Meet with an accountant, take a class on budgeting and invest in budgeting software for your computer and smartphone. Classes for budgeting are available online in many cases, but for those people who need to attend a class in person, they can look for community education courses and contact their local accounting office.

In cases where debts have become too overwhelming to meet a proper financial education, debt consolidation or debt counseling can create a manageable payment plan that will allow an individual to make on-time payments for all of their creditors in one lump sum. Debt consolidation or debt counseling services often have a financial education component included to help prevent financial challenges like this in the future. Take full advantage of these services. Many programs are even free to help individuals who are struggling with their current debts.

How do you know if you should consider a debt consolidation or debt counselor over bankruptcy? While it isn't always as clear cut as looking at the numbers, it is strongly suggested that if your debts are less than one million dollars ($1,000,000) you should not file bankruptcy.

A former real estate investor with six investment properties in foreclosure was able to successfully dispute his foreclosures with the credit bureaus and eliminate all six foreclosures in less than one year. For the common person with only one mortgage in foreclosure, it may seem impossible to recover their credit from such a devastating financial blow. With persistence, knowledge, and a plan you can accomplish anything and make better financial decisions.

Bankruptcy makes getting checking accounts, applying for credit, removing negative items from your credit reports, applying for jobs, being considered for promotions, lowering interest rates, and many other common financial necessities extremely difficult. Before you consider pursuing bankruptcy, exhaust all other methods of recovering from debt and reduce the amount of unnecessary expenses you have.

If you have already filed bankruptcy, you will need to wait until there is no longer any activity in the court or with discharges for a minimum of two years before you can begin disputing items discharged under the bankruptcy. Better Than Credit Repair's dispute process is considered Spring Cleaning and has a specific strategy for removing discharged items and the bankruptcy itself. Follow the step-by-step guide on Spring Cleaning your credit reports for more detailed information in this process.

Your credit profile is made to be flexible and to help you recover from hardships. If you have to consider bankruptcy, there is light at the end of the tunnel and your credit will not be permanently affect by your decision to discharge your debts.

Now that you have the prescription for proper Credit Health, you must create Credit Goals to decide which resources and assets you must be shooting for with your credit. It is vitally important to pay attention to where you are going with your efforts, so lets move on to the next section!

Credit Goals

Earlier in this book, I said there was *one vital thing* missing from your approach to credit that will always keep you *just over broke*. This *one thing* is what makes this process – the development of your personal credit – *Better Than Credit Repair*. It is the goal you set for your credit. The purpose you give your credit is what makes all of the difference. Are you looking for something else to take money away from you, or are you looking for something that changes the tides of your life? To finance something that will pay *you* again and again and again so that your basic needs are always met? What kind of use do you want to get out of your credit?

Have you considered that the one area of our financial lives that we could potentially get the most use from in the shortest period of time is given the least amount of purpose? It may not have dawned on you until now that all of those visions of your future could probably use a credit goal or two because you could achieve them far faster than you could with credit versus saving money from your job to accomplish your dreams. When we think about credit, the last thing we do is determine what purpose we want to use it toward, outside of the abstract idea of just having "good" credit.

After you prove your integrity and credibility to funders, the sky is the limit to the amount of money you will have access to. The mistake most people make is that they use their credit to purchase things they want right now – houses, cars, jewelry, cash advances to spend the money on daily things, you name it – leaving them with tens of thousands and even hundreds of thousands of dollars in debt. What if you could use your debt to create an income for yourself that paid itself off FIRST before racking up more bills to pay and even more liabilities. What about using your credit to create the income that pays for the liabilities that additional bills can bring? That way, your job income is free to do far more for you than before, and your money is actually working for you instead of being funneled into other debt.

When I talk about creating goals, I am talking about far more than your plans on acquiring the next debt in your life. What kind of money do you want to make each month? How much money is your job bringing in for you? What if you could create a resource that brought in the same amount of money your job made and it didn't require you to actually be present for that money to come in? If I had a job that made $2,000.00 per month, my first goal would be to make that $2,000.00 per month independent from my job. Then, my goal would be to double that. Then to triple that. So how can credit help me do this?

Credit allows you the ability to access money that you did not have the access to on your own. Money you can borrow in order to use it more quickly than you would be able to save money to use. If you put $1,000 away every month for a year, you would have $12,000.00 saved. If you opened a secured credit card for $1,000 and paid it on time, you could consolidate your credit cards to create a line of credit of $100,000 a lot faster than saving that $12,000 took you. You could use this line of credit to fund the purchases of assets and collateral that will make money for you. The assets and collateral would be yours and would pay off the loan instead of that money coming from your own pocket.

What is a credit goal?

I have met many people with credit scores in the 700 – 850 range who lack credit goals. They have no target to shoot for with their credit. Most times, they are even afraid to use their credit to be financed for anything, out of fear that their credit will become damaged, or that they are being taken advantage of through paying interest. This is not the behavior of individuals who have reliable credit skills!

Most times, when I talk to these individuals about credit resources and assets - things they can purchase that will add to their income - they are surprised. There was a time when it was common knowledge that your money could work for you instead of you just working for your money.

They simply do not know what resources exist for them, and worse, they believe they can invest money into a passive, risk free business to create resources. There is no such thing as "a passive, risk free business."

Credit Goals create a noble reason to develop your credit resources and assets, and provide a direct course to follow when looking to advance your life.

Why should I have a Credit Goal?

Creating both Major and Minor Credit Goals gives you a blueprint of success for your personal credit.

Credit goals are not the same as goals for your finances in general. Having a savings account with $10,000 in it is not the same as wanting to own your own home. Saving $10,000 has different criteria compared to building 660 + FICO scores and creating a sufficient income to sustain having a home.

As you work to complete your Major Credit Goals, everything keeping you from reaching your Minor Credit Goals is taken away in that process. Before you know it, you have achieved excellent credit and the benefits that you were reaching for.

Another important point about Credit Goals is that you should never have just one, and that you should always seek to increase and advance yourself in whatever credit standing you are looking to achieve.

Credit Profile Education is the successful management and monitoring of your credit reports, credit scores, and the creation of a Credit Profile Showcase to show off your best behavior and credit worthiness. This is what will create the ultimate resources to acquire the lifestyle you are looking for.

Credit Resources & Assets

Going back to my example about my good friend who is living on the brink of disaster, he works really hard for many hours to bring stability to his life with no way to properly protect and secure his basic needs. Neither he nor his wife have assets or resources because they do not believe in using their credit outside of emergencies.

When you use your credit for emergencies and vacations, you create high utilization. You pay the minimum balance every month, often with less than 60% of your card available, and you pay your card off only to make that 60% even worse. You are creating larger problems than you can solve right away and your FICO scores are being heavily impacted.

The purpose of acquiring credit resources and assets is to have money to fall back on. You create assets – things you purchase that add to your income – to create a protection and security for your basic needs if something should happen to your primary income. Your basic needs are the unavoidable expenses and liabilities (things that you purchase that take money away from you) that you use to live. You create resources in order to rely on yourself to fund your goals and dreams versus relying on others to provide that funding for you.

This family has no protections or securities because they do not believe in paying interest. This family does not believe in the development of credit to reduce interest rates. This family has no interest in learning how to play the "credit game" that involves Credit Health – the ability to intelligently manage and care for their credit while making scheduled payments that do not incur interest.

Credit Resources create the ability to build the lifestyle that you desire instead of focusing only on a lifestyle of maintenance and survival.

Assets raise you to the next income bracket because it gives you access to money far beyond what you bring in from your primary source of income.

You have to have favorable personal credit when acquiring large assets. Many times, your regular income or collateral is not enough to purchase assets with the most substantial income production.

If you lose your job, become disabled, or are faced with any other financial strain, your assets replace the income that your job made, protecting your basic needs and sustaining your lifestyle! Now *that's* protection!

So what kinds of assets should you consider purchasing? Study the following list, and research the income producers that you will be passionate about. If you care about what you choose, the more likely you are to care for it properly.

1. Stocks
2. Mutual Funds

3. Bonds

4. Businesses where you can hire others to run them. If you work there, it's your job, not a business.

5. Investment Properties

6. Royalties from music, books, patents or scripts

7. Notes or IOUs

8. Anything else you can be passionate about that produces an income or has collateral value, has a ready market, and appreciates.

As you can see, assets come in a variety of forms. Creating an income from acquiring assets protects your livelihood. Be sure to pick assets that you are passionate about, because passion will ensure that your assets will be taken care of properly.

Credit Resources and Assets will create a financial independence for you and your family. They are a vital part of the use of credit, so do not skip this step.

Now that you have this foundation, you're ready to move on to the proper care of your credit for establishment, restoration and upgrade!

Credit Profile Education

If you knew the three major areas that a funder, lender, investor or anyone else you wanted to borrow money from is going to look at ahead of time, and you had the tools to create the picture perfect image of what they wanted to see, would you want that advantage? Of course you would! Every person is interested in knowing that they can get the results they want. Knowing ahead of time what you need to do to get what you want affords you an amazing opportunity. So how do you master this for your own personal credit? By becoming educated on your credit profile. Educating yourself on how your income, debt ratio and credit scores will impact a funder's decision to lend to you will give you that advantage because those are the three major areas that anyone you borrow from is going to want to know about you.

Credit Profile Education vs. Credit Repair

To best understand how Credit Profile Education and Credit Repair compare, you have to understand what credit repair really is and what it does.

I mentioned earlier in the introduction that companies and individuals offer credit repair services at a standard market price of $500, and it can add up to much more than that if you are paying a monthly fee or paying per deletion. The service itself is comprised of deleting old and untraceable information, updating your personal information and disputing any inaccuracies on your credit reports.

I call this process Spring Cleaning

Spring Cleaning is the process of deleting old and untraceable information, updating your personal information and disputing any inaccuracies on your credit reports.

The most reliable way to spring clean your credit reports is through letter dispute. By writing letters to the credit bureau following a simple template and sending those letters by certified mail, you will raise your credit scores 50 – 75 points in most cases. It creates a paper trail for your disputes, and allows you to follow up based on the last group of letters you sent out.

The information used to dispute inaccuracies in your credit reports involves straightforward statements and references to basic case laws from the Fair Credit Reporting Act, a law that protects our ability to have good credit.

There are two ways that companies and individuals in credit repair determine what should be disputed:

1) Either they make that determination on their own and send you letters to sign and return that they will send out on your behalf, or

2) They ask you to determine what data should be disputed and send letters out on your behalf.

This process is not done by rocket scientists.

Anyone can spring clean his or her credit reports – and the best part is that you typically do a much better job than anyone else can do for you! Why? Because you know much more about your credit report information than anyone else would, and you just need to be guided in the right direction as to what to do to keep your reports from looking unfavorable.

Paying for credit repair is equal to paying a standard market price of $500 for the most basic and elementary first step in the restoration and upgrade of your credit.

That's pretty surprising isn't it? There are even companies that have you pay hundreds of dollars, but they will say that help with credit repair is free and you pay for education! Your real issue is not the very basics of what you need to do to Spring Clean your credit reports. Your issue is the organization process after the Spring Cleaning is done.

When you have no more outdated or untraceable information, what can these companies and individuals do for you?

To be honest, they can't help you with much. Most of these companies and individuals are not equipped with the ability to go any further than Spring Cleaning, and the advice they provide is only to satisfy your immediate desire to be approved. So if you've completed this process before and need to move on to the organization process, you run the risk of paying $500 just to find out that credit repair has no way to help you, and has no idea how to help you with your next steps.

There are companies that provide general ideas as to what

your next steps can be, usually promotions of credit products or auto quotes, in no real order, but providing products still does not show you how to organize a showcase of the wonderful things you do have on your credit.

So what *is* Credit Profile Education?

Credit Profile Education is the process of learning lifetime skills to manage, monitor and maintain your credit profile properly.

First, you need to create a picture of your credit responsibility in order to help a lender make the decision as to how much credit you can receive, if any.

This picture of credit responsibility is formed by understanding that your income, debt ratio and credit scores are what make up your credit profile. When you delete negative and erroneous information from your credit reports, increase the amount of positive credit references on your credit reports, and adopt habits with your payments that produce a larger benefit beyond the immediate benefit you get from that purchase or bill payment, you are focusing on one of each of those three areas. Using debt to create income is also a way to turn the tide of your income in your favor.

Credit Profile Education has 3 parts: Maintenance, Management and Monitoring. These three parts include Spring Cleaning, organizing a Credit Profile Showcase, and the proper use of daily, weekly and monthly habits and schedules to achieve excellent credit.

Creating your Credit Profile Showcase is like creating a job resume. By showcasing the positions that directly compliment what you're applying for, you are reducing the factors that would prevent you for receiving that job. Are you surprised that you have that much control over what lenders and funders see about you? Do you realize that you could have individuals competing for your business because of the way you honor your business relationships?

The better your credit profile is organized, the more trustworthy, reliable and credible you are, and the more integrity you have. Spring Cleaning your credit profile is important because it works to show the best of your credit behavior by restoring what has fallen to the wayside. To do this, you will need to analyze your credit reports to understand what all of that jargon means.

Spring Cleaning gets you familiar with each of the credit reports from the three credit reporting agencies, Trans Union, Equifax and Experian, how they show your information and how to determine what should be cleaned.

When a person has not established credit, it means that there is no record of credit history that has been recorded. Credit history is a record of your credit debt behavior, good or bad, that gives lenders a picture of the kind of risk you are, and shows a picture of trust between you and a lending company.

The three largest credit bureaus, Trans Union, Equifax and Experian, have each created their own credit scores, particularly for their own use. These credit scores are not used by any creditor, funder or lender to determine your credit worthiness, which makes it rather confusing.

When you pay Trans Union and Equifax to see your credit scores, they sell you the credit scores used only for their purposes. These are not the scores that you want.

Although Experian has their own credit score like Trans Union and Equifax, Experian does provide you with the credit scoring model that all lenders, creditors and funders use – your FICO score - when you pay for it.

There are three FICO scores, one for each credit bureau, are they are used by lenders, creditors and funders to determine your credit worthiness. These are the scores you are establishing, restoring and upgrading. You can tell the difference between the credit scores that do not help you and your FICO scores because the words "Officially Certified FICO Score" will accompany them.

A company based out of California called the Fair, Isaac Corporation (FICO) created this model of credit scoring. FICO has created scores for each of the three major credit bureaus to provide the most accurate nationwide reporting of your credit history.

A Credit Reference shows a picture of how responsible you are with your credit debts. Your credit history is reported by each of the three credit bureaus in a credit report. A credit report can be seen as a resume of your credit history, showing your full name and any misspellings, any addresses that you have used, any inquiries into your credit history by other lenders looking to finance you, and all positive, negative and active credit information.

Now that you have a general idea of the way the credit bureaus work, your journey to upgrading your credit can become clearer.

A very important part of your credit profile is your debt ratio. As you acquire credit debts such as credit cards, a mortgage and auto loans, the amounts you owe when added together total your debt ratio. You can offset your debt ratio by adding credit lines from installment loans such as bank loans and credit cards.

You will need to begin adding positive credit references to your credit in order to sway your credit profile toward the excellent credit behavior that you possess.

The following section is a list of Credit References, or credit accounts, that you can add to your credit reports to begin building excellent credit. It is important to reference this sheet when following your guides to establishing, restoring and upgrading your credit, so let's get it out of the way.

Credit References

Because most people are worried about credit debt and being able to delete their previous mistakes, adding credit accounts tends to be one of the most neglected areas on a person's credit report. Most people suffer from imbalance on their credit reports. They have more accounts of one type and not a diversity of accounts that will help them to balance out their types of debt and prevent their credit profiles from showing a false picture of what they're capable of financially.

Credit reports tell someone a lot about the way we live. If you went to school, your school loans will show on your credit reports. If you have medical problems, your credit reports will show medical bills because sometimes we aren't quite able to cover everything. If you have been divorced, your credit report may have a bankruptcy, a tax lien, a car note in default or a mortgage or foreclosure, or a combination of all or any of these. Your credit report tells your life story. By diversifying the types of credit debt accounts on your credit report, you are choosing to tell a different story about the type of person you are. You are choosing to create a showcase for the type of integrity you have instead of being in "woe-is-me" mode; a victim to the whims of life that all seem to appear on your credit when you have difficulties.

So what are some of the different types of credit accounts you can add to your credit profile and how will they help you to create the picture of integrity that you want to show lenders and funders? First, let's start at demystifying what credit references are and how they can help you.

What are positive credit references?

Positive Credit References are credit accounts that you have taken care of extremely well. Their care shows that you are responsible and have integrity and credibility in your finances.

When establishing references, it is important to take into account your debt ratio, and how this credit account will reduce your debt by providing an extension of credit to offset it. How your debt ratio is balanced on your credit reports is very important because it is a determining factor of your approvability for larger resources.

When adding credit references, your household budget is important as well because the additional payments must be accounted for in the money you have available. Remember, credit is supposed to be an extension of the money you have, so do not get carried away. These accounts should be added comfortably to your credit reports without causing a financial strain. Start with one, and do not add additional references until you have your payment schedule timed comfortably through six months of exceptional payments.

Bank Loans – There are two kinds of bank loans. Bank loans that are started with collateral such as cash or items of value are known as secured loans. Bank loans that are provided based upon your income and credit score are called unsecured loans. A credit line is produced based on either of these methods that you can either set yourself or is predetermined.

As you borrow from this credit line to make purchases (like paying your bills, gas and fast food each week) and paying it off immediately with the cash you have on hand for those purchases, you will boost your credit scores and your credit line in the process.

As you pay off what you borrow on your bank loan, you will establish an installment loan history on your credit reports that offsets your debt ratio. As an example, if your total credit debt (debt ratio) is $55,000, and your installment loans are $100,000, your debt ratio becomes $0 and you are worth $45,000!

These loans are important because they grow to create a substantial line of credit for the purchase of assets.

Auto Loans – Auto loans establish a substantial length of credit history, up to 36 months. In order to see a change in your FICO scores, you cannot pay off your auto loan early and you cannot be late on any of your payments.

Paying off your car loan early and making any late payments makes their agreement to raise your FICO score void. If paid on time, your FICO score will be raised. The money you will pay for maintenance, car insurance and other fees is why vehicles are considered liabilities. Auto loans are the only credit reference that

Better Than Credit Repair suggests to pay on time for the duration of the loan. You will receive the benefit of a FICO score boost at the end of the loan period.

Credit Cards – Existing: If you currently have credit cards that you use, you can actually start to raise your scores with them within four months. You need to show that you are not using that credit card as income and that your payments are made frequently each month. Do this in the following ways:

1. If you owe any money on your credit cards, you will need to pay them back to your total line of credit for these cards to be used properly. Pay them down to a zero balance.

2. Make one, $10 purchase each month. This will drop your utilization down to 2%. Do not use your credit card for any other purchases. You must do this for six months.

3. Use your credit card only for purchases that you have the CASH ON HAND to cover – this reduces and could possibly eliminate interest and directly pays your principal, which regular monthly payments based on your minimum balance always avoid.

Credit Cards – Establishing: When establishing credit cards, there are two kinds that you can choose from - unsecured and secured.

1. The typical unsecured credit cards have a limit of $300 - $500 and they pay their own fees out of the card. This means that they may charge you an activation fee, an annual fee, and an assortment of other fees as soon as you

49

open the card. On the one hand, this is good because you will not need to pay these fees yourself to open the card, but having to pay your balance back to $0 from 50% usage can be a financial strain on people with low income. Remember not to fall below that 65% availability on your card.

2. Secured credit cards come from banks. You put $250 - $300 in an escrow account with them, and they will create a credit line off of your money for that amount. Credit cards are an excellent way to create a payment history and boost your credit scores. Use the same techniques that are used for existing credit cards, outlined above.

Important Note: Department store credit cards are not recommended because the interest is too high and they, often times, will not negotiate the interest with you. Remember, the whole purpose of being approved for a credit card is to receive the benefit of growing your credit resource. If you cannot negotiate your interest rates lower and raising your credit scores becomes a challenge, then your benefit is much less than your risk. Department store credit cards are notorious for being high risk.

Merchant Accounts – Available from various retailers online, you can create a line of credit or a merchant account through that retailer that is specific to their particular store. These lines of credit and accounts do not extend out to other stores or retailers and do not come with a Visa or MasterCard logo.

These retailers typically only require you to make purchases from their particular catalog twice per year, although they want you to make more frequent purchases. Your repayment of the line of credit creates an excellent payment history that reports to all three credit bureaus.

Be sure to research these retailers thoroughly before opening lines of credit with them. Not all of these retailers post to any reputable credit bureaus, or they may post to only one credit bureau that is recognized, taking away from your desired benefits. When your benefits are reduced, your risk to your finances becomes higher and your credit scores and credit profile is less likely to improve as a result of adding that account.

Financing Furniture – This, surprisingly, is an excellent way to build a credit reference as well. If you go to a furniture store and finance a small piece of furniture, you will create a record of payment that will show favorably on your credit report. Financing the furniture, and getting a department store credit card are two totally different things. You are not applying for credit with their store, you simply want to make payments on what you are purchasing and have it show on your credit report. Be sure to make that distinction to the sales person.

Piggy-backing on someone else's credit, also known as finding a co-signer – Finding someone to co-sign for purchases can be a challenge within itself. People are taught fundamentally, out of dealing with the consequences of co-signing for irresponsible people, that co-signing is not a good idea.

Generally, it certainly isn't a good idea to co-sign because many people cannot be trusted to protect your credit when they can use it as if it is their own. Their credit is already bad, after all. What do they have to lose?

When someone adds you to his or her credit profile as a co-signer and they have excellent credit, it is sometimes called piggybacking. This method requires a lot of trust because the person who is willing to help is at risk of damaging their credit. The best courses in credit maintenance warn those with excellent credit profiles against becoming a co-signer. This method, however, can certainly be helpful to a person who desires to raise their credit score. In three to six months, credit scores can raise 100 points or better with the help of co-signing.

Co-signers have two main concerns: 1) fraud against their excellent credit (their credit gets misused), and 2) there is nothing in it for them except for the tremendous risk they are taking. There are ways, however, to even the playing field if you decide to ask a person to co-sign a credit card or line of credit for you. The first concern is pivotal to your co-signor's credit care. There are two key techniques to maintaining both your credit and the person who allows you to boost your score by using theirs. This will ensure that no fraud is committed and that their credit will not be misused in any way:

1. Only stay attached to that person's credit for a maximum of 6 months, and

2. *Do not use that person's credit cards or their credit lines*

for any purchases!
Remember, your goal is only to have that person's excellent payment history documented on your reports – *not* to use their credit to make purchases! Using their credit is *wrong*.

A solution to the second concern is to offer your potential co-signor something valuable that you want returned to you for collateral. There are many options that you can choose from, but ensure that what you are offering belongs to you and that you have the right to offer it as collateral.

Some examples of what to use as collateral are:

1) The title to your car
2) Expensive jewelry
3) Electronics that are up to date and in excellent condition
4) The deed to your home
5) Something of your co-signors choice.

Your options for what to use as collateral are endless, and the exchange will be more than worth it when you see the benefits your credit received as a result. Be creative in your desire to thank that person for their help, go far beyond that person's expectations, and you may make a good impression to receive their assistance.

If your co-signor refuses, it is his or her right to do so. Remember, even with collateral, the risk is tremendous on their end and some things may not be worth the exchange to them. The key to developing your credit is to learn how to be responsible so that you do not have to rely on any quick-fix techniques like this to get where you need to be. Responsible credit behavior, making your payments early and organizing your credit profile to showcase your excellent behavior are always the best ways to achieve the benefits you desire.

In the following pages, you will find some handy guides to establish, restore and upgrade your credit.

Easy Personal Credit Development Guides

Credit Establishment

When you have no credit lines or very few, the most important thing for you to do is to establish a proper foundation of Credit Health so that you can properly construct your Credit Profile Showcase.

Writing down what debts you are responsible for in a month will give you an idea of what kind of credit you need to apply for. Begin with a secured credit card and use it to make one, $10 purchase each month to keep your utilization low. As you build your credit card's credit line, you will be able to comfortably fit larger purchases in the 35% utilization amount.

Do you pay rent? Do you pay utilities? What about gas and dining out? As you build your credit lines on your credit cards, each of these personal needs will meet the 35% of your credit line utilization criteria that you want to follow and raise your FICO scores. Many people with unestablished credit do not have the income to sustain owning a credit card, so be sure you have a stable income before applying.

A credit card is not an addition to your income! It is only an alternate avenue for the cash you are using – it produces a resource of larger credit lines so that you can purchase assets to add to your income.

You must determine which credit accounts would be best to add to your credit profile based on your budget. What are your needs? Look at the section on Credit References to get a good idea as to what you should be applying for and remember to only add references that you can afford!

Establish three initial lines of credit - and not all at once! Your first goal is to create regular schedules by adding your credit references to your worksheets from Credit Health. Add a new line of credit after you have kept your schedules regularly for 6 months.

Here are some basic rules to follow when applying for credit references:

1. When applying for credit, do not allow more than three lenders to pull your credit per month. When someone pulls your credit it creates a blemish called an inquiry. More than three inquiries per month will drop your FICO scores and give lenders the impression that you cannot get financing because something may be wrong with your credit profile. The drop in your score can be as much as 100 points from too many inquiries - and it happens *fast*.

2. When adding credit lines – be sure that what you choose to add is something you will get use out of. For example, there are programs available that will allow you to finance a computer without using your credit, but will post positively to your credit reports until you finish paying it off. They have weekly, biweekly and monthly payment

schedules to help you build your credit and receive your purchase quickly. Research these companies and choose one that is best for you.

3. When using credit cards, pay more than your minimum balance. There are two payments that you are making when you pay your credit card bill: 1) interest and 2) principle. Interest is what you are charged above the line of credit that has been lent to you, and the principle is the actual line of credit that needs to be paid back when you use it. Using your credit cards for what you have cash on hand to cover will pay off your principal and keep your interest from increasing.

4. Ensure that the accounts you are adding are raising your FICO scores as well as creating excellent records of payment for you. Use the Credit Health worksheets as well as the credit references in the credit reference section as a guide. You will see a boost in your credit score within 3 – 4 months. Continue to make your payments early and keep track of your Credit Health worksheets and you will enjoy excellent credit in as little time as 3 to 6 months. There is a thin line dividing unestablished and bad credit - keep reading!

Credit Restoration

There are three main areas of focus in Credit Profile Education:

1. Spring Cleaning
2. Organizing your Credit Profile Showcase
3. Upgrading to Excellent Credit

When you have negative entries on your credit reports (which you can have with unestablished or average credit also), the object is to delete the negative entries by disputing inaccurate items and updating your personal information. This is easily done by Spring Cleaning your credit reports.

Companies and individuals that offer credit repair approach the Spring Cleaning process without explaining the process to you. It is recommended that you take charge of the Spring Cleaning process through the development of your personal credit yourself so that you will always know where to begin when you are managing your credit.

As a general rule, entries that are older are easier to remove. Accounts get sold and information gets lost, so it works in your favor to have very old items on your reports that need to come off. The newer an item is, the easier it will be for the credit reporting agencies to verify, and the more difficult it will be to delete. Your newer accounts may need to be settled or have payment arrangements created in order to remove them.

Bankruptcies, repossessions, judgments, tax liens,

foreclosures, and the like are all negative entries that can be removed with a mixture of time and strategy. For example, your first focus should be to delete the negative entries associated with bankruptcy, and when all of those entries are gone, the bankruptcy can be deleted as well. And you don't have to wait seven years. If a bankruptcy has been on your credit for two years or more and has not changed, the process for deletion can begin. This means that the bankruptcy may have been on your credit for three years or longer for the activity to stop. It does not matter what status your bankruptcy is in. So dispute all of your negative credit references, and deal with the tough stuff when it reveals itself through the credit bureau's verification process.

Many individuals suffer as victims of identity theft. This victimization is usually revealed the first time an individual sees their credit reports through unrecognizable personal data or negative entries that were never applied for. The dispute process can be confusing if you cannot verify items as yours. Disputing entries as "This account is not mine" will allow the credit bureaus to properly identify whether the entries belong to you or not, resulting in deletions and a clearer route to follow afterward.

Although you can make disputes on your credit reports online or by phone, disputing negative information by letter is the recommended method through *Better Than Credit Repair* because it creates a paper trail of the disputes that you've made that cannot be denied by the credit bureaus. Your signature, a certified mailing receipt and supporting documents should be included with your dispute letter, ensuring that you have a record of what you sent and when.

You want to be sure your dispute letters are written clearly, simply and include a section of case law from the Fair Credit Reporting Act to reference for the dispute you are making.

Include a copy of your driver's license or state ID card, as well as a copy of your social security card. If you have any pay off letters to prove that you paid any debts, include those with your letter as well.

If the letter is too complicated, the credit bureaus will see your dispute as frivolous and will not follow through. Your letter should never be handwritten, always type it to make it professional and check for spelling and grammatical errors.

If any of this seems complicated, you can find sample dispute letters and dispute letter templates for free online. Finding dispute letter samples to use is easy by doing a simple search online for "free credit dispute letters."

How to Spring Clean your Credit Reports

In order to Spring Clean your credit reports, you need to see what your credit reports look like. You can either order hard copies of your credit reports by phone or you can get copies of your reports online. Every person is entitled to a free copy of his or her credit report once per year. You can also receive free reports if you a) are low income, b) receive public assistance, or c) are denied credit for any reason.

Keep these addresses on hand as you begin your Spring Cleaning to dispute inaccurate information with the three major credit bureaus.

Equifax P.O. Box 740256 Atlanta, GA 30374 (800)-685-1111 Web site: www.equifax.com
Experian PO Box 2002 Allen, TX 75013 (888) 397-3742 Web site: www.experian.com
TransUnion LLC P.O. Box 2000 Chester, PA 19022 (800) 888-4213 Web site: www.transunion.com

10 Steps to Spring Cleaning Your Credit Reports:

1. Call this number to order hard copies of your credit reports: 1-877-FACT-ACT. You will be prompted for identifying information to have your reports sent to you, and they should arrive by mail in 15 days.

2. Isolate your credit references and separate them into "positive" and "negative" references. Each one of your credit accounts has remarks or comments that someone has made about the status of that account.

3. Positive references say "paid satisfactorily," "paid – closed by consumer," or "current" and have excellent payment histories (no late payments).

4. Negative references say "paid," "paid – closed by credit grantor" and they have existing balances (amounts of money that you owe) and have bad payment histories ("30 days late," "90 days late" etc.)

5. You will need to have a confirmation number, file number or report number to reference each of the credit reports you are looking at. Each bureau has a different number for reference, and if you are using online credit reports you may not see it. Feel free to call the credit bureaus to get the number you need to use as a reference number for your disputes. You will need to add this number to your dispute letter.

6. Only send the accounts that you are disputing to the

particular credit bureau that references that negative account. For example, if you have a negative account only showing up for 2 credit bureaus, you only want to add that account to the letter for each one of those bureaus. You will not add that account for the bureau that does not show it.

7. Send your letters by certified mail so that you can have a receipt for when you sent that information.

8. When you are organizing your information to create your Credit Profile Showcase, you do this by making settlements and payment arrangements on the negative accounts that you can handle on your credit reports.

9. When you call to settle, you want to negotiate that the remarks are changed to "paid satisfactorily," "paid-closed by consumer," or "paid – current." You can also negotiate lower interest rates. Also, you can negotiate adding a phrase to the pay-off letter that notifies the credit bureau that your FICO scores be improved once the debt is resolved. Remember, that collection agency is not obligated to raise your credit score if it is not added to the agreement you made in writing. *You must get a letter stating that you have come to this agreement.* This is called a payoff letter. Do not pay by phone and do not pay until you receive this letter. This is very important.

10. Continue this process until you have properly managed

each negative account on your credit reports. It feels good to breathe again doesn't it?

Depending on the amount of positive accounts you have, and whether they will raise your credit scores by practicing credit health, you may need to increase your positive credit references. If you have three credit references that will raise your FICO scores, do not add more at this point. Focus on your Credit Health schedules and making your payments early in order to raise your credit scores.

Make your mortgage payment/rent payments early by 15 days! I cannot stress this enough. A default in your mortgage payment can reduce your credit score by 100 points or more and set your efforts back tremendously! Be extremely diligent about your payment history and make all of your payments early!

You will see significant changes in your credit reports by following these Spring Cleaning and Organization methods. Continue on to the next guide for upgrading your now, average credit.

Average Credit Upgrade

Individuals who have uncertain or high risk credit are the most difficult to convince that their credit can be better than where it is. Achieving and maintaining excellent credit means to take the necessary steps to create excellent credit behaviors, and then to go the extra mile to reach an ultimate credit goal, but if you believe that the way you pay your bills is sufficient, you will never be able to go further beyond where you currently are.

Creating credit goals in order to acquire credit resources and assets is a natural process as you read this book and apply its principles. Achieving excellent credit in order to obtain the best credit resources and assets should be one of your Major Credit Goals to give you the greatest benefit.

As mentioned before, we struggle to become adequate or mediocre with our credit instead of striving to have the best that our credit can offer us out of habit, out of survival and maintaining our current lifestyle. This is different from building a lifestyle that challenges you, meets your needs and provides you with happiness on a daily basis. When we do not strive for more or create goals that challenge us, we become stagnant and we begin to dislike the way we live. We become unfulfilled and our wellbeing and quality of life becomes affected.

FICO sees our credit scores on the following scale:

High Risk 619

Uncertain 620 to 660

Acceptable (average) 661 to 720

Very good 721 or higher

Excellent over 750

The same obstacles that befall a person with no credit and bad credit are the same obstacles that prevent a person with credit in the 619 – 660 range from reaching 800+.

You will need to follow the 10 Steps to Spring Cleaning Your Credit Reports and use the worksheets for Credit Health to reassess your credit behavior in order to begin raising your credit to excellent credit.

You complete the organization of your Credit Profile Showcase by making settlements and payment plans on the negative entries that cannot be deleted. This will prove that you have credibility and integrity by showing you are willing to restore your credit relationships.

Credit Health provides new habits and schedules based on worksheets and the use of consistent daily, weekly, and monthly payments and purchases to boost your credit scores. Go the extra mile of seeking debt management help, household budgeting, and paying yourself FIRST in order to acquire assets and credit resources that will add to your income and totally secure your basic needs.

Your goals are achievable. Start with large goals and then create smaller goals to help you reach the larger goals in manageable steps. Often, we create goals that are far too small for us to reasonably be excited by them and we end up losing the motivation to continue to work on the plans we need to succeed. Challenge yourself! Begin to do the research on the type of assets you need to acquire to produce additional streams of income outside of your job. Choose assets you care about because they will need time to cultivate, and if the assets bore you, you will work on them less. Make goals to replace your job income so that you can work when you want to and not because you have to. This will free up your income and create larger streams of income for you to plan your lifestyle around.

I am passionate about helping others achieve their financial goals with credit as a resource. I turned the mistakes I made into the stepping stones of success for my own personal journey and I can help you to do the same.

Congratulations! You have now received a knowledge base on the development of credit! You have the opportunity to share this information with your family and friends and watch them avoid costly mistakes as they establish, develop and upgrade their personal credit in the future.

Common Questions

1. I can only get one credit report when I order my hard copy credit reports from 1-877-FACT-ACT. What should I do?

    a) If you can't order all three credit reports, you may have already ordered a credit report in a time frame that is too recent to get another copy.

    b) If you are already paying a company to help you with your credit, ask them to send you the most recent copy of your credit reports that they ordered.

    c) You could also access your credit reports online for free on www.annualcreditreport.com and www.creditkarma.com.

2. I don't know what is on my credit reports so I can't answer the identifying questions when they ask me.

    a) Call the 1-877-FACT-ACT number and speak to a representative. They will help you to identify your account in other ways.

    b) If speaking to a representative doesn't work. try to access your credit reports online with www.annualcreditreport.com or www.creditkarma.com.

3. I have way more credit cards than two or three. Should I close my credit cards?

    a) You don't want to close your credit cards, you want to consolidate the balances. Your goal with credit cards is to increase the line of credit so that you can access more funds and have fewer cards doing the work. You don't need 10+ credit cards. Having two or three that do the work of 10 is far better. Single out the two or three cards you like the best.

b) Do not choose department store charge cards. For the "perks" you get for those cards, you could create A LOT more perks with a regular credit card (increased lines of credit, lower interest rates, the ability to negotiate).

c) Call the cards that you want to keep and tell them that you want to consolidate the balances from other cards into that card. They will work with you and tell you how to do it.

4. I have too many credit cards and it is taking all of the income I have to maintain them. What should I do?

a) Consolidate your credit cards. Also, use your credit card to pay what you owe on another card instead of using the money from your job. What is the point of using other people's money if you are still using your own money to cover it? They should be paying for themselves.

5. I'm thinking about financing a car. I don't want to pay a high interest rate but my credit scores are low.

a) Having low credit scores and applying for financing will cost you thousands of dollars more in fees and high interest than you would be paying if you did some work on your credit before financing the car. My suggestion is you work on paying cash for a car and after you are able to work on your credit, finance the car you want at lower interest rate.

b) If you are not able to wait and must finance a car now, work on your credit after you finance the car and negotiate a lower interest rate after six months. Understand that this may be more difficult to do because cars are liabilities – things that you pay for that take money away from you instead of creating more money. You will need to have money for gas, car repairs, insurance, maintenance and incidentals and your car note. Most car financing is a three year agreement, and if you are using your sole income to pay for this car, you could create a brink of disaster situation that may be difficult to recover from.

6. When I ordered my credit reports from the telephone number, I noticed that they do not come with my FICO scores. Why?

a) FICO is an independent company from the credit bureaus and they do not typically provide scores for free with hard copy reports. You can access your FICO scores from www.MyFICO.com for Trans Union and Equifax and you can access your Experian FICO score for free on www.CreditKarma.com. MyFICO.com is not a free website, so you may need to pay to access your FICO scores from there.

b) You could also pay a nominal fee to get your FICO scores from a real estate office. Loan officers will pull your credit for you to see if you qualify for pre-approval and they may allow you to see your FICO scores if you ask them. It may cost a fee for you to see them, but you will be able to see all three scores.

c) Pulling your credit scores yourself does not create a hard inquiry on your credit report, but having a loan officer pull your credit does cause a hard inquiry which can make FICO scores drop a few points.

7. I want to own my own home in a couple years. What is the best way that I can prepare for the process of qualifying for my own home?

a) The more money you have saved for your down payment, the better. You will also need earnest money which is money you can put down on a house to hold it for you. Sometimes this amount is anywhere from $500 - $2,000. You will want to have a minimum of $10,000 as a downpayment for your home also.

b) Two incomes are better than one and the length of time you have been employed is important to lenders.

c) Public records on your credit are amounts that you owe to creditors that have taken you to court and won judgments against you. These can be child support, a lease that was broken and has incurred fees and months of rent due, small claims judgments, tax liens or any other amounts that need to be collected. If you cannot afford to pay these amounts in full, you can go to the county clerk's office where these judgments were incurred, and create a payment plan to take care of them. If you get approved for a house, you will be responsible for paying these public records off before you can close or the amount that you owe could be taken out of your equity for your home. This may not happen in every case, but it is important for you to determine if you have any liens that could come up and potentially prevent you from closing on your home.

8. I received a letter in the mail about a debt that is going to collections. I don't want this debt to end up on my credit report but I couldn't catch it before I received the letter. What should I do?

   a) Call the company and create a payment arrangement with them that will work for your budget.

   b) Do not agree to make any payments by phone. Make sure you can be mailed or emailed a copy of your agreement before making your payments. Ensure that the terms of the agreement on paper are the same as the terms of the agreement you negotiated by phone. Do not make any payments until you see the proper agreement in writing.

9. I did the spring cleaning on my credit reports but there are

three or four negative items that I can't remove. They keep coming back as "verified". What should I do?

a) You may not be able to delete some items from your credit reports because the items have followed the Fair Credit Reporting Act guidelines and are verified as debts belonging to you. If these debts do not belong to you and you have a reason to suspect identity theft, make a police report and report these items as fraudulent.

b) If these debts do belong to you, you can call the number on the collections or look up the account names online and find the number for the companies so that you can make a payment arrangement or settlement. A payment arrangement is your agreement to pay the amount in full with small payments you can afford. A settlement is your agreement to pay a portion of the debt to satisfy the debt in full. Which either arrangement, make sure you get a pay off letter that identifies the terms you negotiated by phone in writing before you make any payments. Do not make payments over the phone because you cannot keep a record of your payment and you do not have the payment arrangement in writing.

c) If you make a payment arrangement, make sure you get a letter stating that on time payments can be reported to the credit bureau to change the payment status to "Paid or Paying as Agreed".

d) Balance is far more important than deleting every negative item on your credit reports right away. If you have stubborn debts that you still need to delete, think about adding positive credit references that will give you a complete picture of balanced good debt so that you can have a healthy credit profile.

10. I want to create goals for my credit and I want to work on the lifestyle that I would like to enjoy, but I think I need to talk to someone to get a better picture of what kinds of goals I should make.

a) You can go to to my website and set an appointment to speak to me one-on-one. I can help you look at what you would like to accomplish and set goals according to what you want your credit to do for you. I can give you a plan to help you develop your credit toward your goal and provide you the tools you need to create a resource out of your credit.

www.ingramcontent.com/pod-product-compliance
Lightning Source LLC
Chambersburg PA
CBHW030903180526
45163CB00004B/1678